SUPER AWESOME FACTS FOR KIDS

RILEY WOLFE

Published by Astro Story Scope.

FREE BONUS

SCAN THIS
AND
GET OUR NEXT BOOK
FOR FREE!

CHAPTERS

DINO DISCOVERIES: UNEARTHING MYSTERIES

This dinosaur is one of the biggest land animals ever! Some people think it might have weighed as much as 100 tons. But did you know that Argentinosaurus actually began its life inside a tiny egg that was about the same size as a football? This means that these dinosaurs grew really fast during their life because they had lots of food and a good environment.

Some dinosaurs, like the Parasaurolophus, had special hollow bumps on their heads that might have made noise. These dinosaurs might have used these sounds to talk to each other, like how many animals today use sounds or songs.

The Woolly Mammoth was a big animal that lived a long time ago during the Ice Age. It had a lot of hair all over its body to keep it warm. This change helped it stay alive in the really tough, cold places during a time called the Pleistocene.

Certain dinosaurs had pointy, curved claws that helped them climb trees. This means that dinosaurs were able to change and live in different places.

The Coelacanth is a really old fish that people thought was gone forever. But guess what? It was found again in 1938! This special creature called a "living fossil" shows us what the ocean was like a long, long time ago.

The Troodon is known as one of the smartest dinosaurs because it has a big brain compared to its body. This dinosaur had a big brain, which means it might have used its smarts more than its muscles to stay alive.

The Tyrannosaurus rex had teeth that were as long as bananas! They were really big, about 9 inches or 23 centimeters long. This means its bite was super strong!

Palm trees started growing about 80 million years ago, when dinosaurs were still around. These special trees are actually more like grass than other trees. They have traveled to warm places all over the world.

The word "dinosaur" comes from Greek and means "scary lizard." This name was made up by Sir Richard Owen in 1842. He used it to describe how big and strong these ancient animals were.

The T. rex had really scary teeth that were made for biting and tearing into meat. This helped it catch big animals and even other dinosaurs. Scientists think the T. rex had the strongest bite force of any land animal ever!

Even though the Stegosaurus was big, its brain was as small as a walnut. Scientists think that these dinosaurs used their pointy tails and strong armor to protect themselves instead of relying on their smarts.

The Compsognathus was a tiny and speedy dinosaur that probably liked to chase after bugs for its meals. This dinosaur was small and fast, which made it really good at catching little animals to eat.

The Dunkleosteus was a really big fish that lived a long time ago. It was one of the strongest hunters in the ocean back then, showing how cool and strong ancient sea creatures were.

Dunkleosteus didn't have teeth like we do. Instead, it had two long, strong blades that could close really fast and with a lot of power. Scientists think that it can open its mouth super fast, in just one-fiftieth of a second! This helps it create a really strong suction force to catch its food. When it shut its mouth, it was so strong that it could crush armor or break bones.

The biggest dinosaur eggs ever found were about as big as basketballs. These eggs were from a group of dinosaurs called sauropods. Sauropods were big animals, some of the biggest ever!

The Dimetrodon was a cool reptile that lived even before the dinosaurs. It had a big sail on its back that helped it stay just the right temperature.

The Eoraptor was one of the very first dinosaurs ever, and it lived a really long time ago, about 230 million years ago. This little dinosaur walked on two legs and liked to eat meat. It helps us learn about how dinosaurs first started to change and evolve.

It was one of the first plants that made forests. Archaeopteris was a cool plant that helped make the air better for animals. It used a process called photosynthesis to take in carbon dioxide and make more oxygen. This made it easier for animals to live on land. The plant's long roots also made soil and helped get rid of carbon dioxide. Even though it doesn't exist anymore, Archaeopteris helped create the forests we see today.

The Woolly Mammoth was a big animal that lived a long time ago during the Ice Age. It had long, curved tusks. These long tusks, which could be as tall as a two-story building, were probably used by the animal for fighting and searching for food in thick snow.

The Titanoboa was a really big snake that could grow as long as 40 feet (12 m). This really old snake, which lived after the dinosaurs died, is the biggest snake ever found.

The Megaloceros, which is also called the Irish Elk, was a really big deer with really big antlers. Even though it was called an elk, it was not really an elk. It was more like a deer that we see today.

The Pachycephalosaurus had a really strong, bumpy helmet on its head that it might have used to fight with. This dinosaur could have used its head to bump into predators or other dinosaurs it didn't like.

A long time ago, a big space rock hit Mexico's Yucatan Peninsula. This made the dinosaurs, flying dinosaurs, and swimming dinosaurs disappear forever.

In the Carboniferous Period, there were really big bugs! Dragonflies had wings that were 2.5 feet long and millipedes were as long as 8 feet. They lived on Earth a long time ago. During this time, there was a lot of oxygen in the air which helped insects to become much bigger than they are now.

The impact would have caused really big waves that traveled all over the world. This caused a lot of animals on land, bigger than a big dog, to die out. Even though something really bad happened, lots of different animals like sharks, jellyfish, fish, scorpions, birds, insects, snakes, turtles, lizards, and crocodiles were able to stay alive.

The Compsognathus was a tiny dinosaur that was really quick. It was about the same size as a chicken. Even though it was small, this creature was probably a really good hunter. It was fast and could move around easily to catch bugs and small animals.

The Dire Wolf was a really big meat-eating animal that lived a long, long time ago when it was super cold. These wolves were bigger and heavier than wolves today, and they probably hunted big plant-eating animals.

The Microraptor was a unique dinosaur with four wings.

It had long arms and legs that worked like wings, just like the wings on birds today. Scientists are still talking about whether it flew like birds or if it was more like a glider, using its wings to go from tree to tree. These really old creatures with four wings can teach us about how flying might have started. They are like a connection between birds and dinosaurs that couldn't fly.

Pterosaurs were not dinosaurs, but they were flying reptiles that lived when dinosaurs were around. Even though they are different, they have a relative in common with dinosaurs and people often think of them together.

The Brachiosaurus had its nose on the top of its head. This special thing, along with its long neck, might have helped it stay cool while eating from tall trees.

The Megalodon, a really old shark, had teeth as big as a human hand. This really big hunter, which could get as long as 60 feet (18 m), was one of the scariest animals in the ocean.

Flowers started growing on Earth about 130 million years ago, when dinosaurs were still around. During this time, called the "Age of Dinosaurs," there were lots of different kinds of plants. These plants helped different kinds of plant-eating dinosaurs to survive.

Scientists recently discovered that Spinosaurus, a type of dinosaur, was actually a semi-aquatic creature. This means it spent a lot of time in the water, which is pretty rare for dinosaurs. This idea comes from finding a Spinosaurus tail that is in really good condition. The tail looks like it was made for swimming, just like a crocodile's tail. If this is true, it would make Spinosaurus one of the coolest dinosaurs because it could live on both land and water.

The Ankylosaurus was a dinosaur that had a lot of armor on its body to protect itself. It also had a tail that looked like a club, which it used to defend itself. This dinosaur had a body covered in hard plates, and its tail could be used to hit predators.

The Megatherium, which is also called the giant ground sloth, was as big as an elephant. This really big animal, which lived a long time ago when it was very cold, is one of the biggest animals that ever lived on land.

The Hesperornis was a really cool bird that loved to swim in the ocean and had super sharp teeth. This bird is a really cool example of how many different kinds of birds there were when dinosaurs were around.

Grass started growing on Earth about 66 million years ago, during a time called the Cretaceous period. This change had a big effect on the environment, giving plant-eating dinosaurs a new kind of food to eat.

Some dinosaurs, like the Velociraptor, had feathers. This means they were probably related to birds.

This discovery also helped us see dinosaurs in a new way. They weren't all scaly, lizard-like creatures like we used to think. Lots of dinosaurs, especially the ones called theropods, had feathers. They looked more like birds than lizards. This is a big change that keeps affecting the study of dinosaurs and how we understand how life on Earth has changed over time.

The Maiasaura is a plant-eating dinosaur that is famous for being a very caring parent to its babies. Fossils show that Maiasaura parents took care of their babies in nests, which is not something reptiles usually do.

Long ago, during a time called the Carboniferous period, the air on Earth had more oxygen. This made it possible for insects and other creepy crawlies to grow really big. During this time, some of the biggest bugs ever lived on Earth.

The Brachiosaurus was a dinosaur with a really long neck. It could grow as tall as 85 feet (26 meters). This dinosaur was really tall and it could walk on four legs. Because of its height, it could eat leaves from trees that other plant-eating animals couldn't reach.

The Archaeopteryx is a special animal that helps us understand how dinosaurs and birds are connected. It has some things in common with both dinosaurs and birds. This animal had feathers and wings like a bird, but it also had teeth and a long, bony tail like a dinosaur.

GALACTIC VOYAGERS: SPACE EXPLORERS

Europa could have a really big ocean hidden under its icy surface. It might be even bigger than all the oceans on Earth put together! Jupiter's strong gravity warms up this moon, making it a cozy place for life to exist. It's kind of like the deep-sea vents on Earth!

Uranus is a special planet because it spins on its side. Scientists think that a really big crash happened in Uranus's history, which caused it to be tilted in a strange way.

A day on Mars, which is called a sol, is 39 minutes and 35 seconds longer than a day on Earth. When we plan what the Mars rovers will do, we remember that there is a small difference in time on Mars compared to Earth.

A day on Mercury is really long because it takes 1,408 Earth hours to complete. This means that one day and one night on Mercury take longer than one whole year on Earth. The year on Mercury is 88 Earth days.

The moon can get really hot or really cold in just a few hours.This happens because it doesn't have a special layer of air to control how hot or cold it gets.

When astronauts go to space where there is no gravity, their bodies feel lighter. This makes their spines stretch out a little bit, so they become a little taller. This is a temporary change, but they go back to their regular height when they come back to Earth.

Astronauts on the International Space Station see 16 sunrises and sunsets every day because they go really fast and are not too close to Earth.

Because there is no wind or water on the moon, the footprints made by astronauts when they went to the moon a long time ago will probably stay there for millions and millions of years. This is a strong reminder of when people first walked on another planet.

Zooming around 250 miles above Earth, there's something really cool called an orbit. It's like a big circle that goes all the way around our planet. It moves super fast, going about 17,500 miles per hour! That's like traveling from one end of the Earth to the other in just an hour. And get this, it completes a full orbit in only 90 minutes.

In 2001, astronauts on the International Space Station got a special treat - they received the very first pizza delivery in space! The pizza was made extra safe and yummy so that it could be eaten in space.

Did you know that Mars has a really long canyon called Valles Marineris? It's so big that you could fit the Grand Canyon inside it 20 times! This big canyon system is more than 2,500 miles long on Mars.

Neutron stars are super dense cores that form when a really big star explodes.

Just one tiny spoonful of their stuff would be as heavy as a huge mountain on Earth! This shows how crazy heavy things can be in space.

The Milky Way galaxy has more than 200 billion stars. That's a whole lot of stars in our galaxy! This number is just a guess, but the real number might be even bigger.

The flag that was put on the moon during the Apollo 11 mission in 1969 is still there, but its colors have become lighter because of the tough moon conditions. This flag represents one of the most amazing things humans have ever done.

Mars has really big dust storms, the biggest in our whole solar system! These storms can go on for months and cover the whole planet. These big storms of dust can make it hard for rovers and other machines to work on Mars.

The sun is really, really big! It's so big that it could hold about 1.3 million Earths inside it. This shows how big the sun is and how it controls everything in our solar system with its strong gravity.

Even though light is super fast, traveling at about 186,282 miles per second (299,791 km per second), if the Sun suddenly disappeared, we wouldn't notice for more than eight minutes. That's because the last bits of sunlight would still be on their way to us.

Even though Saturn is really big, it's actually light enough to float in water if that could ever happen. This happens because it is not as heavy as water. It is made mostly of hydrogen and helium.

Scientists think that the exoplanet 55 Cancri e is mostly made up of shiny crystals that look like diamonds. This happens because it has a lot of carbon and it gets really hot and squished.

Neptune has really fast winds that are the strongest in our whole solar system. They can go as fast as 1,200 miles per hour (1,931 kilometers per hour). These super strong winds are caused by how fast the planet spins and its heat inside.

Some scientists think there might be a really big planet hiding in our solar system. They call it Planet Nine. This made-up planet, if it's real, would help us understand why some things in the Kuiper Belt move in strange ways.

Our home galaxy, the Milky Way, and our space friend, the Andromeda galaxy, are slowly moving towards a really big crash, but it won't happen for about 4.5 billion years.

When they finally meet, it will make lots of new stars appear because the gas clouds will be squished together. But the space between stars is really, really big, so it's very unlikely that stars will crash into each other. In a really, really long time, the two galaxies will come together and become one even bigger galaxy.

Did you know that on a faraway planet called HD 189733b, something really cool happens? It's so windy there that instead of rain falling straight down like it does on Earth, the rain is actually made of glass and it falls sideways! Isn't that amazing? This happens because it's really hot and has strong winds, which makes it very different from Earth.

In 1947, the U.S. sent fruit flies to space to see how space travel affects living things. These were the first living creatures to go to space. The tiny fruit flies were found alive, which is good news for people who want to travel to space in the future.

Black holes are super strong and have a gravity that is so powerful that nothing, not even light, can get away if it gets too close. This makes them really hard to see using normal ways, and we can only find them in a roundabout way.

Pluto spins around once on its axis every 6.4 Earth days. That means that one day on Pluto is like a whole week on Earth. Pluto and its biggest moon, Charon, are always looking at each other because they're tidally locked. If you were on Pluto, there would be a special place where you could see Charon staying still in the sky.

Did you know that Jupiter, the biggest planet in our solar system, has a super cool storm called the Great Red Spot? This storm is even bigger than our whole planet Earth! And guess what? It has been going on for more than 300 years without stopping! This storm is a big part of Jupiter's thick, wild air.

The International Space Station is a really big thing that people made and it's in space. Sometimes, you can even see it from Earth without needing a telescope. It looks like a shiny, speedy dot in the sky at night.

The Milky Way galaxy is spinning really fast, about 168 miles (270 km) every second! Even though our galaxy moves quickly, it still takes a really long time - about 200 million years - to complete one full rotation!

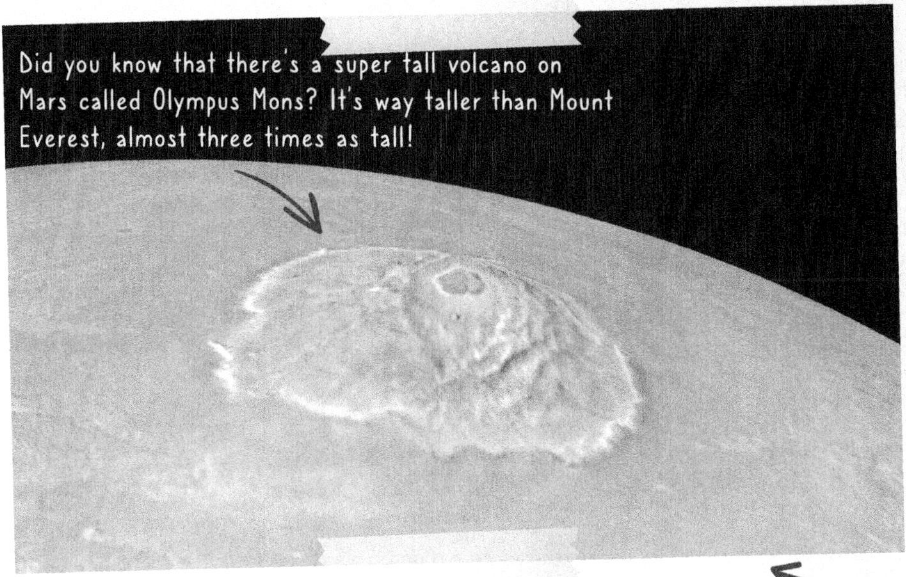

Olympus Mons is the tallest mountain in our whole solar system. It goes really, really high up, about 13.6 miles (22 kilometers). That's almost three times higher than Mount Everest, which is about 5.5 miles (8.8 kilometers) tall.

In the year 2013, a really cool astronaut named Chris Hadfield sang a song called "Space Oddity" by David Bowie. It was the first time ever that someone made a music video in space! The video was made on a big spaceship called the International Space Station. Lots of people on Earth have watched it many, many times.

Haumea is a small planet that is far away from Neptune. It looks like a stretched-out shape and spins around every 3.9 hours. Haumea spins really fast, which makes it look like a stretched-out shape. It's different from other things in space.

In outer space, if two pieces of the same kind of metal touch each other, they can stick together forever. This is called cold welding. This happens because there is no air or water to make a layer of rust on the metal.

Did you know that if we took all the DNA in your body and stretched it out, it would be long enough to go from the Earth to the sun and back about 600 times? That's super duper long! This shows how DNA is very small and holds all the important information about living things.

TIME TRAVELERS: KINGDOMS OF THE PAST

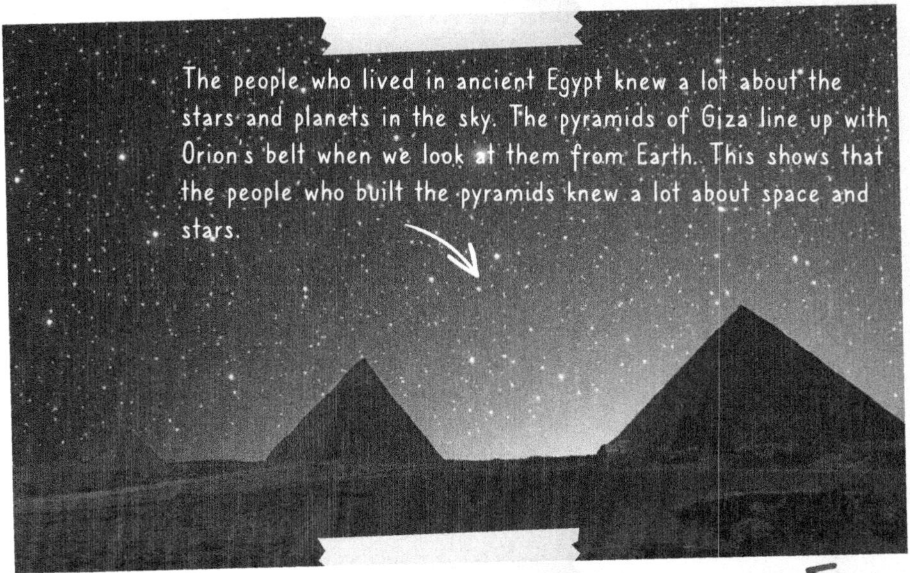

The way the Egyptians lined things up in the sky wasn't just random. They knew a lot about how the stars and planets moved. The ancient Egyptians loved studying the stars and planets. They thought it was a way to connect with the gods and the world around them. Long ago, the people thought that their kings, called pharaohs, went up to the sky when they died. They believed that the pharaohs became gods and lived among the stars.

The word "pharaoh" comes from ancient Egypt and means "big house." At first, it was used to talk about the ruler's palace, but later it started to mean the ruler himself.

The first democratic government in the world was created in ancient Greece. It only lasted for 185 years before a ruler with all the power took over.

Ephesus used to be a very important city in Turkey a long time ago. It was famous during the times when the Greeks and Romans were in charge. The Library of Celsus and the Temple of Artemis are some of the coolest old things you can see there.

The tombs in the pyramids had clever traps to keep thieves away. This shows how much people care about what happens after they die and how they try to protect it.

The Chinese civilization started a long time ago, around 2100 BCE. The Shang Dynasty was the first recorded dynasty, and it lasted from 1600 BCE to 1046 BCE. This group of people is famous for their very old past and important things they did for culture, thinking, and inventions.

Machu Picchu is a really old city that was built a long time ago by the Incas. People sometimes call it the "Lost City of the Incas". It's way up in the mountains in Peru and is a special place that is protected by UNESCO.

Knossos, a place in Greece, was a really important city for the Minoan Civilization. The Palace of Knossos and the Snake Goddess figurine are really cool things from a long time ago.

The famous Egyptian pyramids were not made by slaves, but by skilled workers who were hired to do the job. This goes against what many people believe about how pyramids were built.

Machu Picchu is a special place that sits high up between two mountains. It's called "Old Peak" in a language called Quechua. It's really high up, almost 8,000 feet above the sea! The place was very far away and had lots of tall mountains around it. That's probably why it stayed hidden and safe for a really long time.

Tikal was an old city in Guatemala that was very important to the Mayans. But, sadly, people left the city around 1000 years ago. This city is a really important place for learning about Mayan culture from a long time ago.

The Library of Alexandria was a very important place in Ancient Egypt. It was a big library where thinkers would go to learn and share their ideas. The library had lots of scrolls and books that kept a ton of knowledge.

Petra is an amazing old city in Jordan. It was made by carving rocks and is called the "Rose City" because of its pretty pink color. Petra was built a long time ago in 312 BC and was the important capital of the Nabataean Kingdom.

The city has a really cool monument called Al-Khazneh, which is also known as the "Treasury." It's the star of the show! This amazing building looks like it's protecting the city at the end of a narrow gorge. It's called a treasure house, but it's actually a special tomb made by the ancient Nabataeans. They were really good at building impressive things!

The Babylonians were a really old group of people who lived in a place called Mesopotamia. They were around from a long time ago, starting in the 18th century BCE and lasting until the 6th century BCE. They are famous for making important discoveries and achievements in law, literature, and science.

Tulum, a city in Mexico, was very important in the Mayan Civilization. The old buildings, like the Temple of the Frescoes and the Castle, show us what life was like a long time ago.

Cleopatra, the famous queen of Egypt, was actually from Greece, specifically Macedonia. This fact can be surprising for people who think of her mostly as being from Egypt.

Sitting on top of the Acropolis, which is the tallest spot in the city, the Parthenon is a building that shows how awesome Ancient Greece was at making art and buildings. This temple was made a long time ago, in the 5th century BC. to honor Athena, who was a very important goddess for the city of Athens.

The Parthenon is a very special temple, not like any other! Each of the 46 tall columns in this building was made by the clever ancient Greeks. They built them very carefully so that they look like straight lines, even though they're not. Throughout history, the Parthenon has faced many troubles like disasters and wars. It has been used as a fortress, a church, a mosque, and even a place to store ammunition!

Chan Chan was a very important city in Peru a long time ago. It was part of a group of people called the Chimú Civilization. The Tschudi Palace and the Huaca del Sol are some really cool old buildings that people like to visit.

The really old city of Jericho, in a place called the West Bank, is thought to be one of the oldest cities that people have always lived in. It started way back around 8000 BCE. This city shows how people have lived here for a really long time and have been able to stay strong.

The Persians were a really old group of people who lived in what is now Iran a long time ago. They were around from about 550 BCE to the 4th century BCE. They were famous for having a really big empire and for making cool art, buildings, and rules.

The Egyptian Pharaoh Pepi II had a special way of dealing with flies. He would have slaves put honey on themselves to keep the flies away!

Chichen Itza is a really cool place in Mexico where the Mayans used to live a long time ago. The pyramid has stairs on each side. There are 91 steps on each side. If we add up all the steps, including the platform on top, it equals the number of days in a year, which is 365.

Tiwanaku was a very important place in Bolivia a long time ago. It was a big part of the Tiwanaku Civilization. The ruins of Tiwanaku, like the Gate of the Sun and the Akapana Pyramid, show how amazing it was a long time ago.

The Aztecs were a group of people who lived a long time ago in Mexico. They were around from the 1300s to the 1500s. They are famous for having complicated ways of living together, making decisions, and practicing their beliefs.

El Castillo, the big pyramid at Chichen Itza, is super smart because the people who built it knew a lot about how the stars and planets move in the sky. This pyramid's shape represents the solar year and other things that happen in space. During the spring and autumn equinoxes, something cool happens at the pyramid. When the sun sets, it makes a shadow that looks like a snake named Kukulcan crawling down the steps. It's just an illusion, but it's really neat to see!

Persepolis was a really old city in Iran that used to be the capital of the Persian Empire. It got destroyed by a guy named Alexander the Great in 330 BCE. This city is like a special sign of how amazing the old Persian Empire was. The city's happiness didn't last long because Alexander the Great attacked and ruined it in 330 BCE.

The Mayans believed that having crossed-eyes was special because their sun god, Kinich Ahau, also had crossed-eyes. To make their eyes look different, some people used to hang things in front of their children's eyes. They wanted their eyes to always look crossed.

The Olmecs were a really old group of people who lived in Mexico a long time ago, from about 1400 BCE to 400 BCE. They are often thought of as the first important culture of later civilizations in Mesoamerica.

The Aztecs thought that giving birth was just as important and special as when warriors fought in big battles.

Mohenjo-Daro used to be a very important city in the past. It is now in Pakistan and was part of a civilization called the Indus Valley Civilization. The Great Bath and the Dancing Girl figurine are some of the coolest things you can see in its old ruins.

They thought that when women died while giving birth, they went to the same amazing heavens as men who died in battle. This showed how brave and important it was to bring new life into the world. People used to think that these women joined the special group of people who walked with the Sun as it moved from the highest point in the sky to the horizon at sunset.

Unlike what people today think is beautiful, the Mayans believed that having a big nose was the most attractive thing. People who have smaller noses sometimes wear fake noses made of clay to make their face look different and the way they want it to look.

Long ago, Bagan was the important center of the Pagan Empire. Today, it is a special place in Myanmar with lots of old buildings to explore. There are over 2,000 temples and pagodas that tell stories about the past.

These obsidian blades were even sharper than the super sharp steel razor blades we have today! Some of these really dangerous tools were as tall as a grown-up person. The special obsidian blades were cleverly put into the wooden core. Some were spaced apart, leaving gaps in between, while others were placed close together to make a super sharp edge.

The ancient Romans made a special way to cool their homes. They used water from aqueducts and put it in pipes. This made the air inside their homes feel cooler. These big pipes also brought water for public baths, toilets, fountains, and people's homes. The sewage systems also got rid of dirty water in a good way, by putting it into nearby bodies of water.

The Spanish Conquistadors took over the Mayans and destroyed most of their 10,000 books. But sadly, only a few of them are still around today.

The Phoenicians were a group of people who lived a long time ago in a place called the eastern Mediterranean. They were around from about 1550 BCE to 300 BCE. They are famous for being really good at sailing on the sea and for making one of the first alphabets ever.

The ancient Greeks made a special collar for dogs called a "melium" to keep sheepdogs safe. It had spikes on it! These special collars were made to protect dogs' necks from wolf bites.

Sparta was a really old city in Greece. People there were famous for being very strict and focused on the military. The guys who lived there, called Spartans, spent their lives training for war and following military rules. Sparta was a place where people were really tough and strong. They trained really hard from when they were little kids to be super disciplined, strong, and brave.

Starting at the age of seven, boys went through a tough school program called the 'agoge.' This program was run by the government and its main goal was to train future warriors. The boys learned things like how to be strong and fit, how to survive in different situations, and even how to be sneaky.

Palmyra was a very important city long ago in a place called Syria. It used to be part of a big empire called the Palmyrene Empire. The city had some really cool old buildings that are still standing today, like the Temple of Bel and the Arch of Triumph. These buildings show how amazing the city used to be when it was influenced by both Roman and Persian cultures.

The old city of Carthage, which is now in Tunisia, used to be a very important place in the Mediterranean world. But sadly, the Romans destroyed it during a war called the Third Punic War. This city shows that ancient civilizations always fought for power.

Most shooting stars burn up in the sky, but a few of them, made of strong stuff or bigger in size, make it to the ground as meteorites.

A NASA space suit costs a lot of money, about 12 million dollars. That's because they are very complicated and have lots of high-tech features. These special suits are made to keep astronauts safe in space and help them breathe when they go outside their spaceship.

The speed of light is really fast! It goes about 186,282 miles per second (299,791 km per second). It's the fastest speed we know of in the whole universe. This speed is a very important number in nature and is the foundation of Einstein's theory of relativity.

The moon is slowly getting farther from Earth, like how your fingernails grow. This happens because of something called tidal friction. It also makes the Earth's rotation slow down as time goes on.

Scientists who study space have found a planet that goes around two stars, just like the planet Tatooine in Star Wars. This special kind of system, called a circumbinary system, used to be something people only imagined in stories.

TECHIE TALES: FANTASTIC FUTURES

Amazon was initially called Cadabra, inspired by the magical spell "abracadabra", aiming to bring a touch of magic to the growing world of online shopping.

cadabra

But then, the owner Jeff Bezos decided to change the name because a lawyer heard it wrong and thought it sounded like "cadaver," which wasn't what he wanted for his business. He really liked the Amazon River, which is the biggest river in the world. Because of this, he changed the name of his company to "Amazon." This name represents the many different things he wanted to sell to people all around the world.

In 1978, a person named Gary Thuerk sent the very first spam email. He wanted to sell computers and sent the email to people who used ARPANET. The word "spamming" was made up in 1993 by someone who used the internet a lot.

Myspace used to be a really popular website where people could connect with each other. But something happened when they were moving their information to a new place, and they lost all the stuff that people had uploaded before 2016.

Facebook is blue because the person who made it, Mark Zuckerberg, has trouble seeing certain colors. He chose blue because it's the color he can see the best.

In China, there are some stores that pretend to be Apple Stores. They might sell real Apple products, but sometimes they use fake parts when fixing things.

The @ symbol is used in email addresses because it is one of the symbols on the keyboard that is not used as often. In 1971, a person named Ray Tomlinson created email. He needed a special symbol to separate the username and host without making things confusing.

When Larry Page and Sergey Brin made their search engine, they needed a name that could show how much information they were going to organize. They landed on a place called "Googol," which is a big number with a 1 and 100 zeros after it.

But because someone spelled it wrong during a meeting, "Googol" turned into the famous "Google." The people who started this really liked this cool mistake, so they kept the name. Today, Google is a really important symbol that shows how huge the internet is. The company's main goal is to make it super easy for everyone to find information.

The very first browser was called WorldWideWeb. It was made by a person named Berners-Lee, who is the founder of the World Wide Web. It worked like a browser and an editor.

CAPTCHA is short for "Completely Automated Public Turing test to tell Computer and Humans Apart". It's a way to tell if someone is a real person or a computer program on the internet.

Wi-Fi is not a word made up of letters from other words. Before, it was called IEEE 802.11b, but now it's easier to say Wi-Fi.

Google and Yahoo hired special goats to help take care of their lawns to reduce the amount of pollution they create. In 2009, Google made a deal to bring 200 goats to mow the grass at their Mountain View headquarters.

Every month, more than 6,000 new computer viruses are made and spread in the digital world. This is a lot more than the 50 viruses that were known in 1990.

These tiny bugs can sometimes get into computers through emails. Did you know that almost all emails, around 90%, could have a virus or malware? Lots of people might click on an email or download something without knowing it has a virus. This shows how important it is to have good antivirus software that is always updated. It helps keep us safe from new dangers that are always changing.

Queen Elizabeth II did something really cool in 1976! She became the first royal to send an email. She did this when she visited the Royal Signals and Radar Establishment. She used a special computer network called ARPANET to send an email. This made her the first royal person to ever do it.

The person who made the World Wide Web, Berners-Lee, wishes he didn't put two forward slashes after "http:" in website addresses. He figured out that these things were making people waste time and paper, but it was already too late!

When you feel like your phone is vibrating, but it's not, it's called Phantom Vibration Syndrome.

Long ago, a person who used to work with Air Force missiles said that the password to launch nuclear missiles was really easy. It was eight zeros in a row, and it stayed that way for 20 years. Even though the Air Force says it didn't happen, Blair says it did. They even wrote down the password so nobody would forget it.

Did you know that the Surface Web, which is the part of the internet that search engines can find, is actually a very small portion? It only makes up 0.03% of the whole internet! The rest is called the Deep Web, and it's 400 times bigger.

Reading on a screen makes you read 10% slower than reading on real pages.

Even though the U.S. Air Force said it didn't happen, Mr. Blair still believes what he said. Can you believe that a really dangerous thing like a nuclear missile had a password that was as simple as '00000000'? It's really important to know that security is much stronger now for serious things!

The first Xbox had cool sounds from real space missions!

Did you know that about 86% of people try to put their USBs in the wrong way the first time?

The very first computer virus was called "Creeper" and it was made in 1971. It was like a little test to see how quickly a message could go from one computer to another.

Doctors who played video games for more than three hours a week when they were kids make 37% less mistakes and do laparoscopic surgery 42% quicker.

Guess what? Some people are scared of technology! They have different names for these fears, like Technophobia (being scared of technology), Cyberphobia (being scared of computers), and Nomophobia (being scared of not having your phone).

In our fast-changing digital world, it's not surprising that new fears have come up about technology. These fears are called phobias and they are irrational. Some people get stressed out when they have to use new gadgets, understand complicated machines, or keep up with all the new technology. It's really interesting to see how our brains are changing because of technology! Sometimes it's easy for our brains to keep up, but other times it can be hard.

Amazon's Alexa is a smart helper that listens to you to make things better. It saves what you say in a special place called the cloud.

Nintendo, a company that started in 1889 making playing cards, entered the world of video games in 1977 with the Color TV-Game series. This was when Nintendo started to become a really famous and important company in the world of video games.

The rules for using iTunes say that people should not use their devices to make dangerous weapons like nuclear bombs, missiles, or harmful chemicals.

Every time you see an Apple iPhone ad, the clock on the phone always shows 9:41 a.m. This is the same time that Steve Jobs, the person who made the first iPhone, announced it in the year 2007.

Wikipedia is a big website with lots of information. It has 54 million pages! To make sure everything stays organized and correct, there are 2,456 special computer programs called bots that help out. These bots work hard to keep Wikipedia running smoothly and make sure the information is always accurate and up-to-date.

In 2010, the United States government used PlayStation 3's, but not for playing games!

Did you know that there are more people in the world who have mobile phones than toilets? That's right! Over 6 billion people have mobile phones, while only 4.5 billion people have working toilets.

The U.S. Air Force discovered a smart way to make a supercomputer without spending too much money. They used 1,760 PlayStation 3 consoles, which were already very strong and didn't need a lot of energy. This supercomputer is "green" because it is very powerful and can do difficult tasks like making radar better and working with pictures from satellites. The PlayStation 3 consoles weren't only for playing games. They actually helped with keeping the country safe!

In 1993, a cool astronaut named Aleksandr Serebrov brought a Nintendo Game Boy with him to space on a special mission called Soyuz TM-17.

The QWERTY keyboard layout was made to help typists type without getting their keys stuck on old typewriters. When the letters that are used a lot are spread out, it helps to prevent the keys from bumping into each other. This design is still used today.

Imagine looking up at the dark sky at night and knowing that the little lights that twinkle aren't just stars. They're actually satellites that give internet to people all over the world. This isn't a part of a make-believe movie, but something that's really happening in real life. It's called SpaceX's Starlink project.

Imagine a world where everyone, no matter where they live, can easily use the internet that is really fast. Starlink uses a group of satellites that are closer to Earth than regular ones. Their goal is to give faster and smoother internet service with less delay. They want to help people in areas without internet access. When you look up at the night sky, remember that some of the stars might actually be Starlink satellites. These satellites are part of a cool project that is changing the way we use the internet and showing us new things we can do.

In 2006, there was a special event called a charity auction hosted by Qatar Telecom. During this event, a phone number was sold for a really high price. It became the most expensive phone number ever! The special phone number 666-6666 was bought by someone who wanted to stay secret for a huge amount of money - $2.75 million!

The digital age has changed how American couples meet. In 2017, 40% of couples who got together met online. Guess what? The old way of meeting people through friends became less popular. It went down by 13% from 1995 to 2017.

Google needs a lot of power to run all of its cool services like search, email, cloud storage, and machine learning. It's really amazing! Just in 2020, Google used a really big amount of energy called 15.5 terawatt-hours. To help you understand, this is like using power that is twice as much as what the whole city of San Francisco uses.

Google uses a lot of electricity because their data centers need a ton of energy. Data centers are big buildings that hold lots and lots of computers called servers. These servers do important jobs like handling and saving information for billions of people who use the internet. These machines need to be running and kept cool all the time, which uses a lot of energy. This is important so that the data centers don't get too hot!

The GPS system was first made by the U.S. military, but now everyone in the world can use it for free. But, it costs almost 2 million dollars every day to run.

Google is a really popular website that helps people find information. Every second, about 99,000 people use Google to search for things!

We usually get rid of 90% of the apps we download because they are hard to use, they trick us into paying money, or they take up too much space on our phones.

The three most popular passwords that people use but are not very strong are "123456," "password," and "12345"!

ANIMAL ADVENTURES: INTO THE WILD

This animal can go really fast, even faster than fancy sports cars like the Porsche 911 and the Lamborghini Huracan. It's one of the fastest animals when it comes to going from 0 to super speedy!

The narwhal has a special tooth that looks like a long, twisted horn. It can grow to be as long as 10 feet (3 meters), which is really big! This tooth is different from what other sea animals have.

The woodpecker has a special tongue that wraps around its brain to keep it safe while it pecks on trees. This helps the woodpecker because it lives a special life where it bores holes in trees.

Elephants are really smart! They can look in a mirror and know that they are looking at themselves. This shows that they are very clever.

If a kangaroo's tail is lifted off the ground, it can't jump anymore. This shows how important the tail is for the kangaroo to stay balanced and move around.

The basilisk lizard is really cool because it can run on water! It's so amazing that people even call it the "Jesus Christ lizard".

Flamingos are pink because of the food they eat, like shrimp and algae. This shows how what they eat can change how they look.

The pangolin is a special animal because it is the only mammal that has scales all over its body. These scales make it look like it has armor, which helps keep it safe from harm.

Did you know that a rhinoceros beetle is super strong? It can lift a whopping 850 times its own weight! That's really amazing!

Chameleons can change their color to show how they feel, which is a special way for them to talk to each other. They don't do it to hide, but to show their emotions.

Pangolins have special scales that cover their whole body. These scales are made of the same stuff as our hair and nails, called keratin. They help protect the pangolin from other animals that might want to eat it.

Did you know that a shrimp has its heart in its head? This is something special about shrimps that most other animals don't have.

Did you know that an octopus is a really special sea creature? It has three hearts and its blood is blue! This makes it very different from other animals in the sea.

The mantis shrimp has really amazing eyesight. It can see colors that humans can't see. This helps the mantis shrimp catch its food.

The bumblebee bat is the smallest mammal in the world. It is so tiny that it can fit on the tip of your finger. This makes it a very special kind of animal.

This bat is from Thailand and Myanmar. It lives in caves made of a special kind of rock called limestone. It is very small and weighs the same as a dime. Its body is only about 1.1 to 1.3 inches long.

Ants are super strong, even though they are tiny. They can carry things that are 50 times heavier than their own bodies! This shows how amazing their bodies are.

The star-nosed mole is a really fast eater. It can eat worms so quickly that even humans can't see it happening. This helps the mole because it lives underground.

A kangaroo can't walk backwards, it can only move forward. This shows how special its way of moving is.

The tongue of a blue whale is super big! It's so big that it could fit 50 people standing on it. This shows just how huge the blue whale, the biggest animal on Earth, really is.

This long nose hangs below the monkey's mouth and helps it make loud sounds. The monkey uses these sounds to show it is the boss and to get the attention of other monkeys.

Cows are really good at making friends! They like to spend a lot of time with their best buddy and they have a special way of being social.

Seahorses are really special in the animal world because the daddies are the ones who have babies, which is not very common.

The blobfish looks really sad when it's out of the water, but it actually looks like a normal fish when it's in its deep-sea home. This shows us how pressure can change how an animal looks.

Bats are special because they are the only mammals that can really fly. This makes them different from all other mammals.

Did you know that tapeworms can grow really, really long? They can reach up to 30 feet (9 meters) inside a person or animal's body! It's pretty amazing, but also kind of creepy because tapeworms are parasites.

A bunch of porcupines is called a prickle, which is a perfect name for these prickly animals.

The dung beetle is a tiny bug that can find its way around by looking at the stars. It's really amazing because it shows that even small creatures can be really good at knowing where they are.

This awesome guidance helps them stay on track as they roll balls of poop, which are usually much heavier than themselves, over long distances to save or make a home. Dung beetles are really interesting bugs because they can use the stars to find their way, even though they have small brains. This shows how smart they are at knowing where they are in space. Scientists like to study dung beetles to learn more about how animals find their way around.

The colugo, which is also called the flying lemur, can fly through the air for more than 200 feet (61 m). This is really cool and helps it live in trees.

Even though it looks cute, the slow loris has a bite that has venom. This is rare for mammals and helps them protect themselves.

The boy lyrebird is really good at copying sounds. He can make sounds like other birds and even sounds that people make.

Sloths have a special way of going to the bathroom. They only poop once a week, which helps them save energy.

Koalas love to sleep a lot, sometimes up to 22 hours a day! They do this to save energy.

The horned lizard has a special way to protect itself. It can shoot blood from its eyes to scare away animals that want to eat it. This might seem strange, but it helps the lizard stay safe and survive.

Ostriches have the biggest eyes of any animal that lives on land. This helps them see really well, which is super important for where

Their eyes are about as big as a billiard ball and five times bigger than a human eye! Their height and wide field of vision help them see predators like lions and cheetahs, which is really important for their survival in Africa.

Giraffes don't need much sleep, only about 5 to 30 minutes each day. This is different from other animals.

Penguins can't fly, but they are amazing swimmers! They can glide through the water really fast, even faster than some other water animals.

Did you know that some frogs can freeze in the winter and then come back to life in the spring? It's like they go to sleep and wake up when it gets warm again. This is a very special way that these frogs survive.

The sailfish is a super speedy swimmer in the ocean. It can go as fast as 68 mph (109 kph), which is really, really fast! This helps the sailfish catch its food and be a strong hunter.

Squirrels can't burp or throw up, which is different from other animals. This is because of what they eat and how their tummy works.

Did you know that giraffes have the same number of neck bones as humans? Even though their necks are super long, it's true! It's pretty amazing how different they look from us, but they have the same number of bones in their necks.

Giraffes have a really long neck that can be as tall as eight feet and as heavy as 600 pounds. But guess what? They only have seven neck bones, just like us humans! But, unlike our bones, their bones can grow to be as long as 10 inches.

The bombardier beetle has a special way to protect itself. It can shoot really hot chemicals from its bottom to scare away enemies. It's surprising, but it works well!

Owls can move their necks in a really cool way! They can turn their heads up to 270 degrees, which helps them catch their food.

Boy peacocks show off their pretty and colorful feathers to find a girlfriend, which is a way animals choose their partners.

A grizzly bear has a really strong bite. It's so strong that it could crush a bowling ball. This shows how powerful and strong grizzly bears are.

Crocodiles are really old! Some of them can live for 100 years, which is a really long time. They are one of the reptiles that live the longest.

The mimic octopus is really good at pretending to be other animals. It can change how it looks and what color it is to blend in with its surroundings. This helps it hide from other animals and stay safe.

Did you know that a bunch of jellyfish is called a smack? It's a funny name that shows how they all move together in the water.

Did you know that when a cat purrs, it can actually help our bodies heal? It's pretty amazing! The sound vibrations from a cat's purr can help fix our bones and tissues. So next time you hear a cat purring, remember that it's not just a happy sound, it's also good for our health!

When a cat purrs, it makes a special sound that can make bones and muscles stronger, just like when you exercise. This happy sound can also make you feel less worried, help you breathe better if you have trouble breathing, and even make your blood pressure go down. It's like having a furry little doctor!

Did you know that snails can sleep for a really long time? They can actually sleep for up to three whole years! This just goes to show how relaxed and slow-paced their lives are.

Dogs have an amazing sense of smell that is much better than ours. This helps them find people in search and rescue missions.

Did you know that some ants have a special way to protect their colony? They can explode themselves! It may sound strange, but it's true. These ants are very selfless and will sacrifice themselves to keep their colony safe. This is a great example of how insects can help each other.

SUPERSTAR SPORTS: GAMES & GLORY

There are many reasons why there are so many balls. Sometimes, they get kicked into the stands or damaged during the game. They also need to be checked if a team thinks there is too much air inside.

Aroldis Chapman is a really fast baseball pitcher! He holds the record for throwing the fastest pitch ever, going as fast as 105.1 mph (or 169.1 km/hr). This amazing thing happened in 2010 when Chapman was playing baseball for the Cincinnati Reds against the San Diego Padres.

Senet is a really old game from Egypt that was played a long, long time ago. It's actually the oldest board game ever! The game was played on a grid with 30 squares. The squares were arranged in three rows of ten. In the game, you moved pieces based on the roll of a dice.

In 2012, a really big game of dodgeball happened with 6,084 people playing! That's a lot of players! The University of California, Irvine planned a big event and beat their own record from before.

Jacob Matlala, also known as "Baby Jake," was a really short professional boxer. He was only 4 feet 10 inches tall, which is about 147 centimeters. In fact, he holds the record for being the shortest boxer ever! Even though he was small, Matlala did really well in his career and won lots of big prizes.

Soccer, which is also called football, is played by around 270 million people all over the world. This sport is loved by both people who play it professionally and those who play it for fun. It is the most popular sport in the whole world.

In Spain, a really big human pyramid was made in 2016. It had 1,202 people in it! The event was put together by a group called Castellers de Vilafranca. They love to build towers with people, which is a special tradition in Catalonia.

The longest tennis match ever happened at Wimbledon in 2010. It lasted for 11 hours and 5 minutes! John Isner and Nicolas Mahut played a really long match that lasted for three whole days! In the end, Isner was the winner.

The best score you can get in one game of bowling is 300 points. To get this score, you have to knock down all the pins with a strike for 12 turns in a row. Getting a perfect score is really hard and doesn't happen very often. It takes a lot of skill and a little bit of luck.

In Catalonia, there is a fun tradition where people make tall towers by climbing on each other's shoulders. In Catalan culture, there is a special celebration that shows how important it is to work together and be a team. It's called "the practice." During this celebration, people come together to enjoy music and have fun!

The fastest tennis serve ever was hit by Samuel Groth. It went really, really fast at a speed of 163.7 miles per hour or 263.4 kilometers per hour! This amazing record was made during a big competition in Busan, South Korea, in 2012.

In 2015, a person named Freddy Nock from Switzerland walked on a tightrope very high up in the French Alps. Can you guess how high? It was 11,669 feet above sea level, which is like being on top of a really tall mountain!

Freddy walked on a tightrope between two tall mountains. The tightrope was really long, measuring 1,138 feet (or 347 meters). Freddy didn't wear a safety belt, even though there was a really long drop from the tightrope to the ground.

Chess is a really old game that started in India a long time ago. People all over the world play it now. The game is a fun board game that two people can play. It's played on a board with 64 squares in a grid shape.

In 1989, a really big game of musical chairs happened with 8,238 people playing. The event happened in Singapore and was put together by the Singapore Sports Council.

In Scotland in 2019, there was a really, really long soccer game that lasted for 108 hours and 2 minutes! Can you imagine playing soccer for that long?

In 2016, a really big game of capture the flag happened. It had 2,888 people playing! The game was played by the University of California, Irvine, in California, USA, on September 22, 2015.

Did you know that golf balls can go really fast? They can be hit at speeds up to 170 miles per hour, which is about 274 kilometers per hour! The golfer's strength and technique, along with the special design of the golf club and ball, help them hit the ball really fast.

For example, Tiger Woods, who is really good at golf, swings the club really fast at about 120 miles per hour (that's 193 kilometers per hour). He can hit the ball really far because he swings really hard and knows how to do it just right. How fast you swing the golf club is really important because it affects how the ball flies, how far it goes, and how well you do in the game.

The biggest game of Twister ever played was on a super huge mat that was 171 feet 3 inches long and 158 feet 5.5 inches wide (52.19 meters x 48.29 meters). This really big game happened at the AT&T Stadium in Arlington, Texas.

In 2019, a really big game of tag happened with 10,908 people playing! It was shown on Fischer's YouTube channel, which has over 5.8 million people who like to watch it.

The biggest score you can get in a game of Scrabble is 830 points. In 2006, a guy named Michael Cresta set a really cool record while playing a game in Massachusetts, USA.

There are only two days every year when no professional sports games happen. This is the day right before and right after the Major League Baseball All-Star Game.

In 2007, a really big game of Simon Says happened. It had 12,215 people playing at the Utah Summer Games Opening Ceremony in Cedar City, Utah on June 14, 2007.

Basketball was created by a teacher named James Naismith from Canada in December 1891. He used a soccer ball and two peach baskets to make the game.

These baskets didn't have a hole at the bottom, so whenever someone scored a goal, someone had to climb up and get the ball. Naismith made a list of the important rules for the game, like dribbling and passing, and put it up on the wall in the gym. The game became popular fast and changed over time to become the sport we play now.

The very first Daytona 500 race happened on February 22nd, 1959. Guess what? It took a really long time, 61 whole hours, to figure out who won because the race was super close and they had to look at a photo to decide! Lee Petty won the race and later became the dad of the famous race car driver, Richard Petty. This was the start of the Daytona 500's cool story.

The University of California, Irvine - ASUCI, played the biggest game of red light / green light ever on September 21, 2022, in Irvine, California, USA. A huge number of 1,415 people joined in, and the school's mascot, Peter the Anteater, helped control the traffic.

Usain Bolt, a really fast runner from Jamaica, went as fast as 27.8 miles per hour (44.7 kilometers per hour) when he ran the 100-meter race at the World Championships in Berlin in 2009. That's the fastest anyone has ever run!

A person named Veronica Torr from New Zealand ran really fast in a race called the 100-meter hurdles. She finished in only 18.523 seconds! What's even more amazing is that she was wearing swim fins while running. She made this record in Beijing, China, on a TV show called Zheng Da Zong Yi-Guinness World Records Special on December 8, 2010.

Horse racing started a long, long time ago, around 4500 BC. Even the Greeks began racing horse-drawn chariots and two-wheeled carts around 1000 BC.

Wilt Chamberlain once scored the most points ever in a basketball game. He got 100 points in a game in 1962!

In the past, a long time ago, around the year 664 BC, something special happened. It was during a special event called the 33rd Olympiad. Horse racing, which is a sport where people ride horses really fast, became an official sport! The people who rode the horses were called jockeys, just like they are today. The Romans

In 1974, a man named Mike Austin hit the longest golf drive ever! He hit the ball really far, and it traveled 515 yards (that's like 470 meters!). This amazing record happened at a big golf tournament in Las Vegas called the U.S. National Seniors Open Championship.

A guy named Aleksander Sapic from Serbia is really good at playing water polo. He scored the most goals ever in one season of the Water Polo World League. He scored an amazing 56 goals in the 2005 season.

Soccer, also known as football, started a long time ago in China with a game called "cuju". A game called cuju was played a long time ago, over 2,000 years ago, during the Han Dynasty. In this game, players tried to score goals by kicking a leather ball through two bamboo canes that were placed close together.

The players kicked a ball made of leather. They tried to kick it between two sticks made of bamboo. These canes were placed quite near each other, only about 11 to 16 inches (30 to 40 cm) apart. That's about as wide as a big computer screen!

A person named Wasilja Peterse from the Netherlands has a really cool record. They were able to knock down a huge number of mini dominoes - 3,202 of them! This cool thing happened in a place called Arnhem, in a country called the Netherlands, on September 15, 2020. It all started because someone saw a really cool domino show on TV way back in 1999 and got inspired.

In 2010, a really big game of hide-and-seek happened with 1,437 people playing! The event was put together by a group called the Jiangsu Broadcasting Corporation in a city called Nanjing, which is in China.

The people who made Monopoly, called Hasbro, say that the longest game ever played lasted a super long 70 days! Sadly, we don't know much about this marathon gaming session. We don't know when or where it happened.

Baseball used to be played in England a long time ago, even before it became popular in America.

The game we play today started a long time ago in English villages. People used to play games like rounders and stoolball, which are similar to the game we know now. These fun games with bats and balls, like cricket, were played by grown-ups to have fun, but then kids started to love them too. When the games traveled across the ocean to North America, they changed and became more popular, turning into the sport we now know as baseball. Then, in 1845, a man named Alexander Cartwright in New York City made some rules for the game and the rest is history!

On July 25, 2010, a really big space hopper race happened with 771 people at a place called the Don Valley Grass Bowl in Sheffield, England, UK.

The largest Rock, Paper, Scissors contest ever had 10,033 players. Tianjin Joy City in China planned a special event from December 21 to 24, 2019. They were celebrating their 8th anniversary!

Barry Bonds is really good at hitting home runs! He has the record for hitting the most home runs in one season and in his whole career. In the year 2001, he hit 73 home runs, which was more than Mark McGwire's record. Then, he broke the career record by hitting 762 home runs, which was more than Hank Aaron's previous record of 755.

UNDERWATER EXPLORERS: OCEANS OF FUN

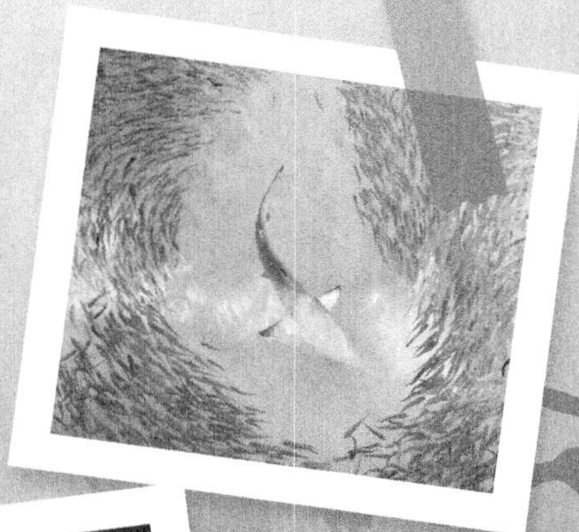

The blue whale is a really big sea creature. It can grow up to 100 feet long (that's as long as 30 meters!) and weigh as much as 200 tons (that's 181 metric tons!). It's even bigger than the biggest dinosaurs that ever lived on Earth!

Did you know that a blue whale's heart is really big? It's so big that a person could actually swim through its arteries! Even though they are big, these gentle giants mostly eat tiny shrimp-like creatures called krill. They can eat as much as 4 tons of krill every day when it's time to eat.

The Colossal squid has the biggest beak of all squids. It uses its beak to catch and eat its food. This creature that lives in the deep sea is the biggest one without a backbone. The largest one ever found was about 16 feet (4.8 m) long.

The electric eel can make a big zap of electricity, like a shock, that is as strong as 600 volts. It uses this zap to surprise its food and scare away animals that want to eat it.

The stonefish is a very dangerous fish that lives in the ocean. It is really good at hiding on the ocean floor and surprising its food. The fin on its back has sharp spines that have a strong poison!

The Christmas tree worm is called that because it has pretty, curly gills that look like the branches of a Christmas tree. These cool worms live in the ocean and are often seen on coral reefs. They are famous for their super bright colors.

The narwhal is a special sea creature that is sometimes called the "unicorn of the sea." It has a long, twisty tusk that makes it unique. This long tooth, called a tusk, can grow up to 10 feet (3 m) long. It is usually found in male animals.

Did you know that some sharks, like the hammerhead, have a cool organ called the ampullae of Lorenzini? This special organ helps them detect electrical fields.

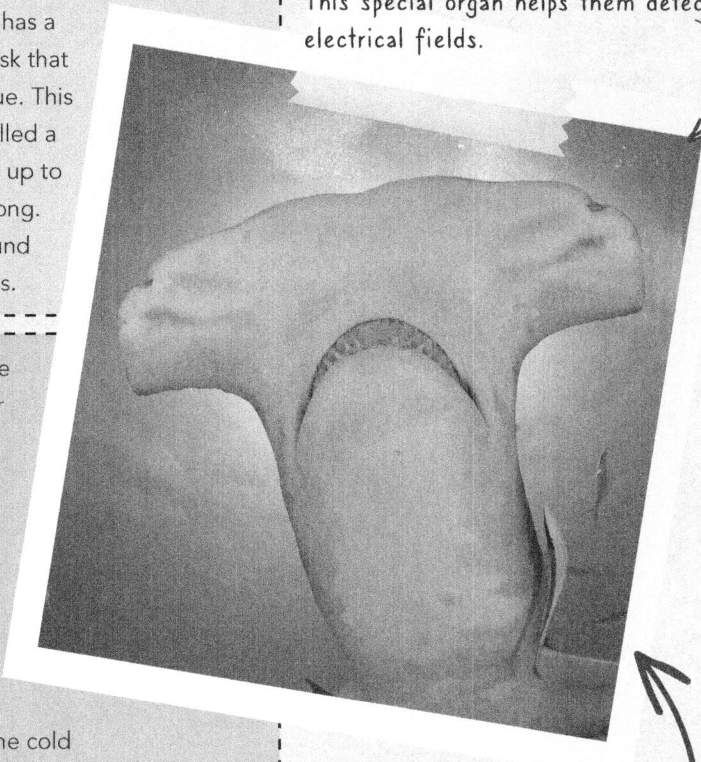

Sea otters have the thickest fur of any animal. They have up to 1 million hairs in just one square inch! This thick fur helps them stay warm in the cold waters of the Pacific Ocean.

Their wide, flat heads help them detect electricity over a large area. This helps them clean the ocean floor and find hidden prey, like stingrays hiding in the sand. Sharks are really good at hunting because they have a special ability and a super strong sense of smell.

The Pacific barreleye fish has a see-through head, which means it can see through its own skull. This special ability helps it find food and enemies right above it in the dark ocean depths.

Did you know that some types of sea turtles, like the loggerhead, can stay underwater without taking a breath for as long as 5 hours? They do this by making their heart beat slower to save oxygen. Sometimes, their heart only beats once every nine minutes.

The Mariana Trench is a really deep part of the ocean in the Pacific Ocean. It's the deepest part of all the oceans in the world, going down more than 36,000 feet (10,973 meters).

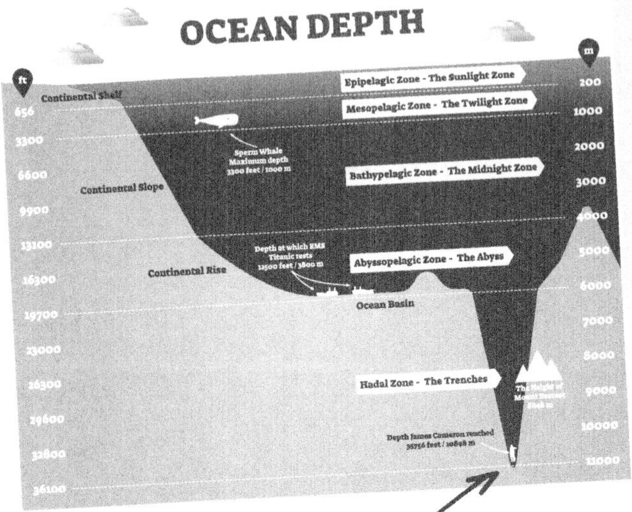

The Greenland shark is a type of shark that moves very slowly. It can live for more than 400 years, which is a really long time! This means it is one of the animals that can live for a very long time on Earth.

The Mariana Trench is a place deep in the ocean that has a lot of pressure, like the surface of Titan. It's also really cold, like Mars. And it's always dark there, just like space. It's kind of like being on another planet! The fact that life can survive in tough places suggests that there might be life on other planets or moons with really tough conditions, like the deep oceans on Europa or Enceladus.

The mantis shrimp is a cool sea creature with super strong claws. It can hunt really fast, like a bullet! This super fast attack is really strong! It can break the walls of a glass tank and is used to crack open the shells of the food it eats.

Humpback whales have the longest flippers out of all the whale species. They can grow up to 16 feet (4.8 m) long. These long flippers, which can be as long as one-third of their body, help them move better in the water.

The giant squid has the biggest eyes of all animals. They can be as wide as 10 inches (25 cm). The squid has really big eyes that help it see in the deep, dark ocean where there isn't much light.

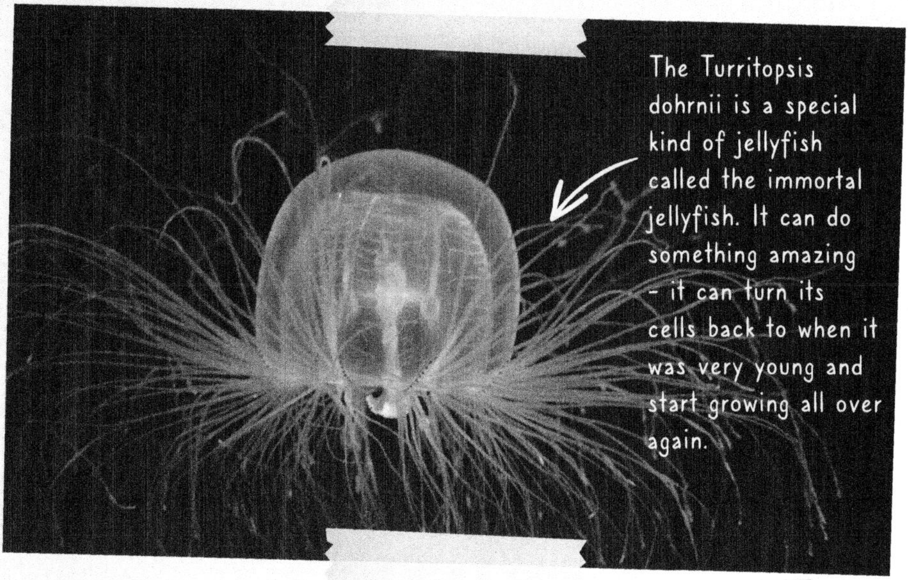

This cool process is called 'transdifferentiation'. It allows the jellyfish's cells to change what they do, making the jellyfish turn back into a young jellyfish called a 'polyp'. Even though this trick helps the jellyfish not die from getting old, it can still be killed by other animals or sicknesses. But scientists are still very interested in this special ability to start over in life.

Did you know that there are rivers and lakes underwater in the ocean? They are created because of differences in how salty and warm the water is. These special pools of water under the sea are called brine pools. They are very thick and can even look like a lake or river, just like the ones we see on land.

The Pacific Ocean is the biggest ocean on Earth. It is even bigger than all the land on Earth put together! It's really big! It has more than half of all the water in the world and is even bigger than all the land on every continent put together.

The frilled shark has more than 300 teeth that are organized into 25 rows. This creature is sometimes called a "living fossil" because it has very old-fashioned features and hasn't changed much for millions of years.

Coral reefs are made up of lots of little animals called coral polyps. These polyps work together to build the reef over a really long time, like thousands of years. These special places called "rainforests of the sea" are like underwater jungles.

The Portuguese man o' war is not just one creature, but a group of little creatures called zooids. They all work together as a team.

These special creatures called zooids need each other to survive. When they join together, they become a powerful life-form that can swim in the big ocean, catch food, and make more of themselves. The Portuguese man o' war is a special sea creature that has a really cool body structure. It's a great example of how working together and having different jobs can help them survive in the tough ocean.

The sawfish has a long, flat nose with sharp teeth that it uses to cut through its food. This special tool can find hidden prey in the sand by sensing their electrical signals. It has small sensors that can feel the signals.

The box jellyfish is a very dangerous creature that can hurt people because it has a strong poison. The tentacles have lots of special cells called cnidocytes. Each cell has a tiny, barbed thread that can give a strong venom.

The dumbo octopus is a special kind of octopus that has fins that look like ears. It uses these fins to help it swim in the deep ocean. This creature lives really deep in the ocean, about 22,000 feet down. That's as deep as 7,000 meters! It's one of the deepest living species we know about.

The Great Barrier Reef is a really big living structure in the ocean near Australia. So big, that you can see it from space! This big coral reef is super long, stretching over 1,400 miles (2,300 kilometers). It's a home for lots of different sea animals and is one of the seven natural wonders of the world.

These creatures live in oceans all around the world. They are known for having a big difference between boys and girls. The girls can grow up to be 6.6 feet tall (2 meters), while the boys are only about an inch long (2.4 cm). This big difference in size is one of the most noticeable in the animal world.

Sea cucumbers have a special way to protect themselves from enemies. They can push out their insides to scare away predators. Once the danger is gone, their bodies can grow back these body parts in just a few weeks.

The mimic octopus is really good at pretending! It can change how it looks, what color it is, and even how it acts to copy other sea creatures. This special power helps it stay away from dangerous animals and sometimes tricks other animals into coming closer.

Clownfish and sea anemones are really good friends! They help each other out and live together. The clownfish keeps the anemone safe from bad guys who want to eat it, and in return, the anemone gives the clownfish a cozy place to live. The clownfish has a slimy layer on its skin that keeps it safe from the anemone's stinging cells.

The deep-sea dragonfish has a special light on its chin that it uses to catch food in the dark ocean depths. This deep-sea predator has special lights on its belly to hide from other predators that are below it.

This big event where lots of animals have babies helps make sure the species doesn't die out. Sunfish are really big fish! They can weigh as much as a car or even more. Some sunfish are as heavy as 5,000 pounds, which is super duper heavy! Even though sunfish are really big, they won't hurt people and eat things like jellyfish, small fish, tiny plants, and algae.

The leatherback sea turtle is the biggest. It can weigh as much as 1,500 pounds (680 kg). It's from other turtles because it doesn't have a hard, bony shell. Instead, it has a soft, leathery shell called a carapace, which is why it's called a leatherback.

The ribbon eel is a special kind of eel. It can change its color and even its sex as it grows up! They start off as boy eels with black bodies and a yellow fin on their back. But as they grow up, they change colors and become girl eels.

The vampire squid has big, red eyes and arms that look like webs. It can use its arms to wrap around its food. Even though it's called that, it doesn't eat blood. Instead, it eats the stuff that falls to the bottom of the ocean, like garbage. That's why people call it the "garbage collector of the sea."

The deep-sea hatchetfish is called that because it looks like a hatchet, which is a tool with a thin, flat blade. These special fish can make their own light! They use this light to hide from big fish that want to eat them.

They use their pointy beak to grab fish from the water, and they have special spines on the top of their mouth and tongue that face backwards to help keep the fish from slipping away. The spines on the fish's body are like a special lock. They stop the fish from slipping away when the puffin opens its beak to catch more fish.

About 70% of the Earth's surface is covered by water, mostly in the form of big oceans. This is super important for controlling the Earth's weather and has lots of different kinds of animals and plants. We still have a lot to learn about all the cool things that live there.

The pistol shrimp is a cool creature that can make a big boom to catch its food. It snaps its claw really fast and makes a big wave that stuns its prey. This thing makes a bubble that, when it goes away, makes a really loud noise that can hurt or even kill little fish.

The anglerfish has developed special ways to catch its food. It has a special thing on its heads that looks like a lure, which helps them attract their prey. This special glowing part of the anglerfish looks like smaller animals, tricking fish and squid into coming close so the anglerfish can eat them.

Did you know that in seahorse families, it's the daddy seahorse who gets pregnant and has the babies? The mommy puts her eggs in a special pocket on the daddy's tummy. He takes care of them and helps them grow until they are ready to come out.

YUMMY JOURNEYS: EXPLORING FLAVORS

Ostriches are the biggest birds in the world. They lay the biggest eggs out of all the bird species. Their eggs are really big, each one is about as big as a cantaloupe and weighs as much as 3 pounds! Inside, there's enough room to hold as much as 24 chicken eggs.

Chili peppers have something called capsaicin in them. This special thing makes your mouth feel like it's burning because it attaches to the parts in your mouth that feel pain. Your body reacts to spicy foods just like it does to physical heat. That's why spicy foods can feel really hot and even hurt a little.

Even though water doesn't go bad, the bottles it's kept in can get old and release chemicals into the water. Did you know that the date you see on a bottle of water is not for the water inside, but for the bottle itself?

Raspberries are yummy fruits that taste sweet and a little sour. They are part of a big family called Rosaceae, which also has roses, strawberries, and apples. This big family has over 2,000 different types of animals.

Lobsters used to be thought of as food for poor people and were even eaten by prisoners in the olden days. But now, they are seen as a fancy treat that not everyone can afford. As time went by, there were fewer and fewer lobsters. But as people found better ways to travel, lobsters became a fancy food that people really like to eat.

If you think coriander, which is also called cilantro, tastes like soap, it might be because of a special gene that affects how you smell and taste things. This thing affects about 4-14% of people, depending on where their family comes from.

American cheese, which is often seen as squishy, yellow slices, isn't actually considered real cheese.

It's made from a mix of Colby and Cheddar cheeses, milk, and different things added to give it color. This food melts easily and is good for you because it has protein and calcium. Sometimes it's called "American singles" instead of "cheese".

Honey is a super strong food that never goes bad because it doesn't have much water and has a special acid in it. Did you know that archaeologists found pots of honey in really old Egyptian tombs? These pots are more than 3000 years old and guess what? The honey is still good to eat!

Some foods like ranch dressing or coffee creamer have something called titanium dioxide in them. This is a special ingredient that makes things look white. It's also used in things like paint, plastic, and sunscreen. This stuff is added to food to make it look better and more yummy.

The red color in Skittles comes from a special kind of beetle. The beetle's bodies are crushed to make a dye called carmine or cochineal. This special coloring has been used for a very long time and is found in many different foods and beauty products.

Pineapple plants are special because they only make one fruit at a time. But it takes them a while, about two to three years, to grow that fruit.

Did you know that one pineapple plant can make yummy fruits for up to 50 years? These plants may grow slowly, but they are very strong and determined. They keep producing their yummy and tangy fruits for 50 years!

The pound cake is called that because it uses a pound of flour, butter, eggs, and sugar in the recipe. This baking tradition started a long time ago in Europe in the 18th century. People in the Americas liked it because it was easy to do and had ingredients that were easy to remember.

The Aztecs used cacao beans, which are the main thing in chocolate, as money. They were very important because it took a lot of hard work to grow and make them into chocolate.

Nutella is a yummy spread made of chocolate and hazelnuts that people love. It uses a big chunk of the hazelnuts that are grown in the world. This actually affects how much hazelnuts cost all around the world.

Doughnuts got their name from a clever way of baking invented by Elizabeth Gregory. To make sure the dough cooks all the way through, she put nuts in the middle of the dough before frying it. That's why they're called dough-nuts.

In the 18th century, people in Europe thought tomatoes were poisonous. They even called them "the poison apple."

The fancy people, who used special plates, sometimes got sick after eating tomatoes because the acid in the fruit made lead from the plates mix into their food. This made them have lead poisoning. The tomato was unfairly accused of causing these bad things to happen.

Honey comes in lots of different colors. Some honey is very light and almost see-through, while other honey is really dark brown. The honey can have different colors because the bees visit different flowers for nectar. Each flower has its own special pigments that make the honey look different.

Even though they're called French fries, they actually came from Belgium. People there used to fry little fish, and that's how they got the idea to make fries! Long ago, when rivers turned into ice during winter and there weren't many fish to catch, people came up with a clever idea. They took potatoes and cut them into long, thin shapes. Then, they cooked them in hot oil until they turned crispy and delicious. And that's how French fries came to be!

Salmon that is raised on a farm starts off being a light greyish-white color. But then, it is dyed pink to make it look the way people expect it to look. Wild salmon get their pink color from eating small animals called crustaceans. These are not something that farm-raised salmon eat.

Chicken wings were usually thrown away or used to make soup until a lady named Teressa Bellissimo made something called Buffalo wings in the 1960s. She owned a restaurant called Anchor Bar in Buffalo, New York.

This yummy food is usually eaten with celery and blue cheese or ranch sauce. It's made by frying the wings without any breading and then covering them in a sauce made with vinegar and spices. It became very popular and was used a lot at bars, restaurants, and parties all over the country. This yummy creation changed the way Americans snack and made chicken wings a popular choice for appetizers and parties.

Did you know that the inside of a banana peel can help stop the itchiness from a mosquito bite? This relief comes from oils in the peel that are found in nature. These oils can help reduce inflammation.

White chocolate is not considered real chocolate because it doesn't have cocoa solids, which are an important part of regular chocolate. Instead, it's made from cocoa butter, milk solids, and sugar. These ingredients make it creamy and sweet.

Good-for-you foods, like yummy fruits, veggies, and lean proteins, can be way more expensive than not-so-healthy foods, like fast food or ready-made meals. The difference in cost can make it hard for people to eat healthy.

In the olden days, people thought ketchup could help with tummy troubles like diarrhea, indigestion, and jaundice. They even sold it as a medicine! This happened because people thought tomatoes were good for your health.

Did you know that apple pie, which is a yummy dessert loved by many people in America, actually came from Europe a long time ago? People from England, the Netherlands, and Sweden have been making apple pie recipes for a really long time, even before the United States existed.

Thomas Jefferson, who was the third president of the United States, is often said to have made pasta popular in America.

After visiting Paris, he brought back the very first macaroni machine to the United States. He also made his own pasta machine. Thomas Jefferson introduced macaroni and cheese to America, and it has had a big influence on the food we eat.

Did you know that about 60% of the genes in humans are also found in bananas? This shows that humans and bananas have a lot in common because we share a history of evolution. However, the things that genes control are usually very different in humans and bananas.

The Popsicle was accidentally made in 1905 by a kid named Frank Epperson who was 11 years old. One time, someone left a mix of powdered soda and water outside with a stick for stirring. They forgot about it and it got really cold overnight. When they checked on it the next day, they found out that it had frozen and turned into the very first Popsicle!

Even though Russia has been drinking vodka for a long time, they only decided that beer is an alcoholic drink in 2011. In the past, people thought that beer and other drinks with less than 10% alcohol were like food.

During the Middle Ages, black pepper was a very special and valuable spice. People even called it "black gold."

Black pepper was really popular and valuable back in the 15th and 16th centuries. People wanted it so much that they started exploring the world to find new ways to get it from India, where it grew. This time was called the Age of Discovery because Europeans were discovering new places in their search for black pepper.

Crackers can actually cause cavities faster than candy! Crackers have stuff called starch that turns into sugar quickly and stays on teeth longer than the sugar in candy.

Blueberries are really good for you! They have lots of things called antioxidants, fiber, and vitamins K and C. Eating them can make you healthy and strong.

Caesar salad is not actually from Italy! It was created by a person named Caesar Cardini in Mexico in 1927 who made a special dish on the Fourth of July when he was very busy. He used the ingredients he had left in his kitchen.

Most bananas we eat are actually copies of each other! They are all the same kind called Cavendish. They are made by a special way called vegetative reproduction. This process helps bananas always taste and look the same, but it also makes them more likely to get sick.

Did you know that potatoes can soak up and bounce back radio waves, just like how people can? It's pretty cool!

In 2012, Boeing wanted to make their in-flight wireless connection better. To test it, they put sacks of potatoes in the seats instead of real people. The project had a funny name, SPUDS, and it helped them make Wi-Fi signals better in different airplanes.

Good-for-you foods, like yummy fruits, veggies, and lean proteins, can be up to 10 times more expensive than not-so-healthy foods, like fast food or ready-made meals. The difference in cost can make it hard for families and kids to eat healthy, even when they want to!

Pineapple has a special stuff called bromelain that helps break down proteins. If your mouth feels tingly or like it's burning when you eat pineapple, it might be because you're extra sensitive to something called bromelain. Bromelain is like a special ingredient in pineapple that can start to break down the proteins in your mouth and on your tongue.

MARVELOUS MONUMENTS:
A GLOBAL TOUR

There's a small town in Norway called "Hell," and it experiences freezing temperatures during the winter months.

The word "Hell" comes from an old word called "hellir" in a language called Old Norse. "Hellir" means a cave that is found under a cliff or an overhang. It doesn't have anything to do with the English word for the place where bad people go after they die. But that doesn't stop people who speak English from laughing about the cold weather in a place called "Hell."

Capela dos Ossos is a special chapel in Portugal. Inside, the walls are decorated with human skulls and bones. A monk named Franciscan built the chapel a long time ago in the 16th century. He wanted to teach people that life doesn't last forever.

The Chocolate Hills are a cool thing in the Philippines. They are big hills that look like chocolate. They are in a place called Bohol. There are lots of hills, more than 1,260 of them! They become brown when it's not raining, and that's why they're called that.

Venice, Italy, is a special city made up of over 100 tiny islands in a lagoon in the Adriatic Sea. It's called "The Floating City" because it doesn't have any roads, only canals.

Mount Everest is a really tall mountain in the Himalayas. It's the highest mountain in the whole world! The mountain is really tall, reaching 29,029 feet (8,848 meters) high. Lots of people like to climb it because it's a big challenge and a cool place to visit.

Did you know that there is a really big beaver dam in Canada? It's in Wood Buffalo National Park and it's over 2788 feet (850 meters) long! It's really big that you can see it from outer space.

The Amazon Rainforest is really thick, so when it rains, it takes a long time for the water to reach the ground, sometimes up to 10 minutes!

The Grand Prismatic Spring in Yellowstone National Park, USA, is one of the biggest hot springs in the world. This place is famous for its bright colors! The colors come from special bacteria that live in the water and make pretty mats.

Pig Beach is a special island in the Bahamas called Exuma. It doesn't have any people living on it. It's famous for a group of wild pigs that live in the water and play with people who visit.

When rain falls in the rainforest, it takes some time for the water to reach different parts of the forest. This creates many small homes for different plants and animals. These homes have different amounts of water, heat, and sunlight. The Amazon has lots of different plants and animals, which makes it a really special place. It's known for having a huge variety of living things!

The Sahara Desert is the biggest hot desert on Earth. Stretching across many countries in North Africa, this place is as big as the United States. It covers an area of 3.6 million square miles (9.3 million square km).

The Colosseum in Rome, Italy, is the biggest amphitheater ever made. This big place could hold around 50,000 to 80,000 people. It was used for exciting gladiator fights, fun shows, and cool plays.

Vatican City is a tiny country inside Rome, Italy. It's the smallest country in the world, both in size and in the number of people who live there. It's really tiny, like it could fit inside Central Park in New York City.

Central Park is really big! It covers about 843 acres, which is almost eight times bigger than Vatican City. It's a really tiny place, only about 110 acres or 0.17 square miles. But even though it's so small, it's still considered its own independent country! The city-state has around 800 people living there, which is much smaller than lots of small towns!

The Great Sphinx of Giza in Egypt is a really big and really old statue. It is 241 feet long and 66 feet tall. This cool statue was made a long time ago, about 4,500 years ago. It has the body of a lion and the head of a person. It was built when Pharaoh Khafre was in charge.

The Eiffel Tower is a famous building in Paris, France. It's really easy to recognize because it looks different from other buildings. Some famous people in France didn't like how it looked at first, but now it's really famous and lots of people visit it.

The Bermuda Triangle is a place in the ocean where ships and airplanes have gone missing. It's in the western part of the North Atlantic Ocean.

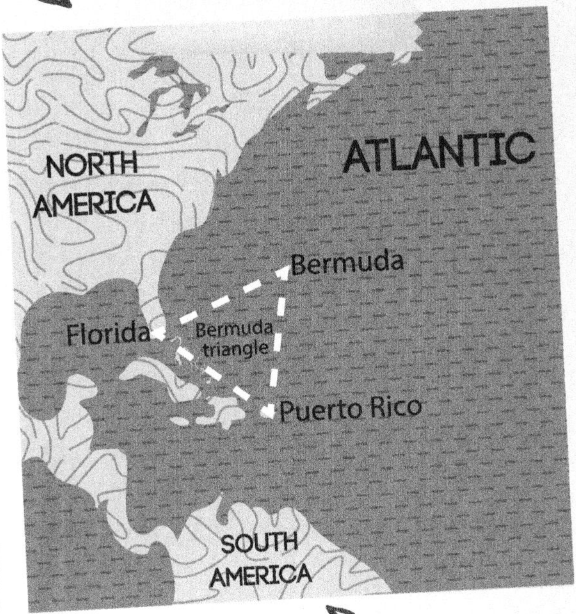

Even though some people think ghosts or aliens are involved, most scientists believe that these disappearances are caused by things like the weather and the Earth's features.

Nowhere -> No place Else is a tiny town in Tasmania, Australia. It's in the countryside and not very crowded. Because of its unique name, this place is very interesting and lots of people like to take funny pictures there.

Lake Victoria is a really big lake in East Africa. It's the biggest lake in Africa and the second biggest freshwater lake in the whole world! It's really big! It can hold enough water to fill up all the bathtubs on Earth.

Eisriesenwelt is a really big ice cave in Austria. It's the biggest one in the whole world! It goes for more than 26 miles (42km), and the first mile (1.6 km) is covered in ice.

Istanbul, Turkey is a special city because it is in both Europe and Asia. This is because it is in a very important spot. The city is split into two parts by a special place called the Bosphorus Strait. Because of this, people who live in or visit Istanbul can have a really cool experience. They can be in two continents at the same time! This is something that makes Istanbul special.

Shani Shingnapur is a special village in India where the houses don't have doors, only door frames. The bank in our town doesn't have locks because everyone trusts and believes in each other.

Methuselah is a really old tree called a bristlecone pine. It lives in the White Mountains in California. It's super special because it's like a time capsule that's still alive. This tree is really, really old! It's been around for more than 4,800 years, which is even older than the Great Pyramids of Giza!

Giethoorn is a special village in the Netherlands. It's in a place called Overijssel. What makes it unique is that instead of roads, there are lots of waterways. The village is sometimes called the "Dutch Venice" because it has lots of canals and cute houses with thatched roofs.

The tree's yearly growth rings are like a special book that tells us about the environment for over 4,000 years. This really old tree called the bristlecone pine is super tough. It can handle really bad weather and keep away bugs because of its strong and sticky wood. Methuselah's exact spot is a secret so it stays safe, just like special places that have old things buried in them.

The Galápagos Islands are a group of islands in the Pacific Ocean. They have a special kind of tortoise that can live for more than 150 years. These islands are really cool because they have lots of different animals that you can't find anywhere else. They even inspired a scientist named Charles Darwin to come up with a really important idea about how animals change over time.

Florida is the flattest state in the U.S. It doesn't have many hills or mountains. The highest point in Florida is called Britton Hill, and it's only 345 feet (105 meters) above the level of the ocean. This makes the land in Florida even flatter than a pancake.

Saint-Louis-du-Ha! Ha! is a special town in Quebec, Canada. It's the only place in the whole world with two exclamation points in its name! This special name shows how fun and exciting the town is!

The Dead Sea is a really salty body of water. It's found between Jordan on one side and Israel and Palestine on the other. The water has a lot of salt, which makes it easy for people to float on top.

Angel Falls in Venezuela is the tallest waterfall in the world without any breaks. This amazing sight in South America is really tall! It's 3,212 feet (979 meters) high and has a big drop of 2,648 feet (807 meters). People think it's really cool to see!

The Taal Volcano in the Philippines is the smallest active volcano in the world. Even though it's not very big, this volcano in the Philippines is really busy! It has erupted 33 times!

This super salty sea is about ten times saltier than the regular seawater you'd find in the open ocean. The sea is the lowest part of the Earth's surface. It is more than 400 meters below sea level. This makes the air special and helps protect us from the sun's rays. It also has lots of oxygen, which is good for our health and can help our skin too.

The Great Barrier Reef is a really big coral reef system. It's found off the coast of Queensland, Australia. The Great Barrier Reef is made up of more than 2,900 separate reefs and 900 islands. It stretches over a distance of 1,400 miles (2,200 km).

The Caribbean Sea has around 7,000 islands. Some of the islands you can visit are Cuba, Jamaica, and Puerto Rico. If you visited one island each day, it would take you more than 19 years to see them all.

When little creatures in the water called dinoflagellates get bothered by something like a wave, they start to glow in a beautiful blue color. This is called bioluminescence, which is what makes fireflies glow. It's a cool trick for these little creatures to try and scare away anything that might want to eat them.

The Great Wall of China is the longest thing that people have ever built. It is really long, stretching over 13,000 miles (21,196 km). It goes through different types of land and weather.

Did you know that there is a really big shoe in Marikina, Philippines? It is the largest shoe in the whole world! This shoe is over 17 feet long and 8 feet wide, which is about 5 times longer than a regular shoe and twice as wide. Marikina is a special place in the Philippines because it is famous for making lots of shoes. People even call it the shoe capital!

Salar de Uyuni is a really big flat area made of salt in Bolivia. It's the biggest one in the whole world! Covering an area of 4,000 square miles (6,437 sq-km), this place is a big home for many types of flamingos. It's also an important place where we find a special kind of material called lithium.

The Grand Canyon is a really big hole in Arizona, USA. It was made by a river called the Colorado River. The thing is really long, about 277 miles (446 km), and it can be as wide as 18 miles (29 km). It's super cool and one of the most amazing things in nature!

The Door to Hell is a special place in Derweze, Turkmenistan where there is a lot of natural gas. The field has been on fire since 1971 when scientists accidentally set it ablaze.

It happened when some scientists accidentally made a hole in a cave filled with natural gas, and then the cave fell down. To stop the poisonous gases from coming out, they lit it on fire, thinking it would go out fast. But it's still burning now, and that's why it has a scary nickname. The bright, always-burning fires have made it a surprising place that lots of tourists like to visit.

The Leaning Tower of Pisa in Italy is really famous because it leans to the side by accident. The leaning of the building started a long time ago when it was being built in the 12th century. This happened because the ground on one side was too soft and not strong enough. As time passed, the leaning has gotten worse and worse.

Son Doong Cave in Vietnam is the biggest cave ever! It is really long, more than 5.5 miles (8.8 km) long. Some parts are really tall, reaching up to 656 ft (200 meters) and really wide, 492 ft (150 meters). It lets you see an underground world that not many people get to see.

MASTERMIND INVENTIONS: GENIUS GADGETS

The Wright brothers, Orville and Wilbur, made the very first airplane. They flew it for the first time on December 17, 1903 in Kitty Hawk, North Carolina.

The very first flight, flown by a guy named Orville, went for 120 feet (which is about 36 meters) and lasted for 12 seconds. They did four flights that day. The longest one was 852 feet (260 meters) and it lasted 59 seconds. It was a small start to the time when people started flying.

The very first microwave oven was made in 1946 by a clever engineer named Percy Spencer. He worked at a company called Raytheon Corporation. Percy found out that microwaves could cook food when a candy bar in his pocket melted.

The very first bicycle was made by a person named Karl von Drais in 1817. It was called a "running machine" or "dandy horse." It didn't have pedals, and the rider used their feet to push it along.

A long time ago in 1770, a clever person named Edward Nairne, who was from England and worked as an engineer, made the very first rubber eraser.

The very first potato chips were made by a chef named George Crum in 1853. He worked in a place called Saratoga Springs, New York. One day, a customer told him that their fries were too thick. So, George decided to make something different and sliced the potatoes really thin. And that's how potato chips were born!

The very first digital camera was made in 1975 by a clever engineer named Steven Sasson. He worked at a company called Eastman Kodak. The thing weighed 8 pounds (3.6 kg) and it took 23 seconds to take one picture.

The very first 3D movie, called "The Power of Love," came out in 1922. To see the cool 3D effects, people had to wear special glasses with red and green or red and blue lenses.

Did you know that the very first recipe for popcorn was discovered in a really old tomb in Peru? People think it's more than 6,700 years old! The seeds found in the tomb were in such good condition that they could still turn into popcorn.

These special glasses have lenses that are either red and green or red and blue. When you wear them, each eye sees a different picture. This makes things look like they are popping out and gives the illusion that they are three-dimensional. This was an old version of the 3D technology we know now.

The very first chocolate bar was made in 1847 by a person named Joseph Fry. He found out that if he mixed melted cacao butter with Dutch cocoa, he could create a chocolate paste that could be shaped into a bar.

The very first crayons were made by two people named Edwin Binney and C. Harold Smith. They owned a company that made paint called Binney & Smith. Later on, their company became known as Crayola.

The very first roller coaster was made in 1884 at a place called Coney Island in New York. It was inspired by the old railroads that used to carry coal down mountains.

It was easier than the roller coasters we have now with lots of fancy technology. It was made of two wooden tracks that went down 600 feet (183 m) at a slow 6 mph (10 kph). People would go up to a high platform and ride in a car along a track. Then they would switch to another car to go back to where they started.

The first modern trampoline was made a long time ago in 1936 by two guys named George Nissen and Larry Griswold. Both of them were gymnasts and they wanted to use the trampoline to practice doing flips.

The very first eyeglasses were made in Italy around 1290. Believe it or not, we don't know who exactly invented them.

The very first zippers were made a long time ago in 1893 by a person named Whitcomb Judson. He made them to help people with their shoes.

The very first calculator that used the power of the sun was made by a company called Sharp Corporation in the year 1978. The calculator was called the EL-8026. It had a special solar cell that helped power it, along with a battery.

A man named John Logie Baird made the first television in the 1920s. Old televisions used to be different from the ones we have now. They had a special spinning disk with holes that helped make the pictures we see on the screen.

They used a special spinning disk with little holes in it. This disk would look at a picture, one line at a time. The light from the picture would go to a special sensor that changes the light into an electrical signal. Then, the signal was sent to another device that could make the picture again. This simple technology was the start of the TV we have now.

The very first vacuum cleaner was made in 1901 by a clever person named Hubert Cecil Booth. The machine was named "Puffing Billy" and it had an engine. But instead of moving on its own, it needed horses to pull it.

A long time ago in China, a clever monk and mathematician named Yi Xing made a special clock. It was the very first clock that didn't need anyone to wind it up.

The very first vending machine was made by a clever engineer named Hero of Alexandria. He was from Greece and he created it a long, long time ago in the first century. When you put a coin in, it gave out special water that is blessed.

In 1913, a person named Fred W. Wolf from Fort Wayne, Indiana made the first refrigerator that actually worked. It was called the "Domelre," which stands for DOMestic ELectric REfrigerator.

In 1973, a man named Martin Cooper, who worked for a company called Motorola, made the very first phone call using a special phone called the Motorola DynaTAC. This phone was pretty heavy, weighing about 2.2 pounds (1 kg).

You can only use it for 30 minutes before it needs to be charged again. Charging it takes a long 10 hours! Even though it took ten more years for this phone to be sold to everyone, its invention in 1973 changed everything. It was a story about a time when people could talk to each other no matter where they were, not just at home or work.

The first version of the internet, called ARPANET, was made a long time ago in the late 1960s and early 1970s. It was created by the U.S. Department of Defense.

In 1971, a clever computer programmer named Ray Tomlinson sent the very first email. He used the "at" symbol to separate the user's name from the computer's name.

The ice cream cone became really popular at a special event called the 1904 World's Fair in St. Louis, Missouri. At the fair, an ice cream seller ran out of bowls to serve his ice cream. Luckily, he found a waffle seller nearby and they decided to use rolled-up waffles instead. People loved it! And that's how the ice cream cone was born.

In 1881, a really smart person named Alexander Graham Bell made something called a metal detector. It's a special device that can find metal things hidden in the ground. He made it to look for a bullet stuck in President James Garfield after someone tried to hurt him!

Surfers in California made the first skateboard in the 1950s. They wanted to ride on land like they do on waves when there are no waves to surf on.

The very first jigsaw puzzle that people could buy was made in 1908 by a person named Archie McPhee. It was called the "Super Fun Puzzle" and had 500 pieces.

In 1868, a special light was put up outside the Houses of Parliament in London. It was called a traffic light and it helped people know when to stop and go while they were driving. The light was powered by gas and a police officer had to turn it on and off by hand.

In 1893, two people named George Schneider and Albert Marsh made the first electric toaster. It was called the "Eclipse" and could only toast one side of the bread at a time.

The ice cream cone became really popular at a big event called the 1904 World's Fair in St. Louis, Missouri. There was an ice cream seller who ran out of bowls, so he asked a waffle seller nearby if they could work together. They came up with the idea to put the ice cream in a rolled-up waffle, and people loved it!

It became really popular right away! People loved that they could eat the container after they finished their ice cream, so there was no trash left behind. This cool and clever idea changed how people ate ice cream and became popular all around the world. Today, it's really hard to imagine having a yummy scoop of ice cream without the special cone.

In 1908, a person named Alva J. Fisher made the very first electric washing machine. It was named the "Thor" and it looked like a big wooden barrel.

The very first ballpoint pen was made in 1938 by a person named László Bíró. He was a journalist from Hungary and Argentina.

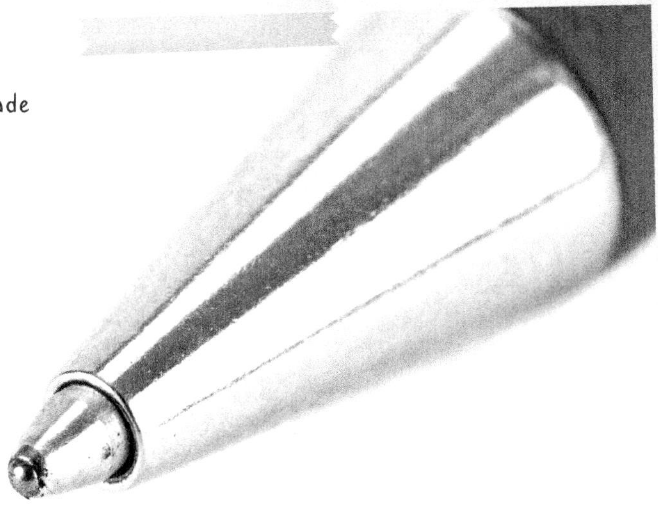

He made a small ball inside the pen that can spin around. When you write, the ball spins and takes ink from the cartridge onto the paper. This means the ink dries fast and doesn't make a mess. Biro's invention was a really big hit and even now, we still use "biros" for writing every day!

The very first photocopier, called the Xerox 914, was made in 1959 by a clever person named Chester Carlson. There was a special way called xerography that used electricity to make pictures on paper. It used a special kind of paper that could hold tiny colored particles. The electricity made the particles stick to the paper, and then they were heated up to stay on the paper.

Toilet paper was first used a long time ago in China, around the 6th century. But it wasn't until the 14th century that a lot of it started being made.

Henry W. Seeley invented the first electric iron in 1882. It was called the "electric flatiron" and it made ironing clothes super easy!

A long time ago, in 1845, a clever inventor named Stephen Perry from Britain made the very first rubber band. Rubber bands were first made from a special kind of rubber called vulcanized rubber. People used them to keep papers or envelopes together.

A man named Jesse W. Reno made the very first escalator in 1891. It was a fun ride at the amusement park called the "inclined elevator."

Reno's design for escalators was very different from the ones we see today. Instead of steps, there was a slanted platform that moved and had a surface that was not slippery. People would stand on this special platform and it would lift them up into the air. It became very popular right away, and then engineers made changes to Reno's design to create the escalators we have now. Did you know that escalators were first made for fun at fairs? So, the next time you ride one, remember its fun beginnings!

The electric blender was made in 1922 by someone named Stephen Poplawski.He wanted to make it simpler to mix yummy milkshakes!

Did you know that the very first chewing gum was made by a man named John B. Curtis way back in 1848? This gum is called "State of Maine Pure Spruce Gum" because it is made from the sap of the spruce tree.

Did you know that the very first recipe for s'mores was written down in a book for Girl Scouts way back in 1927? The book called "Tramping and Trailing with the Girl Scouts" had a recipe for a yummy treat called "Some More." People started calling it "S'mores" for short.

Dear reader,

First and foremost, I want to express my heartfelt gratitude for choosing my book to share with your family. I sincerely hope that you have found joy, learning, and inspiration within these pages.

As an author, I pour my heart and soul into creating books that not only entertain but also provide valuable experiences. Your feedback is incredibly important to me and helps me to continue creating content that resonates with readers around the world.

If you enjoyed reading this book I kindly ask you to consider leaving a review.

I want you to know that I will personally read each and every review. Your thoughts mean a great deal to me. To make this process as seamless as possible, I have included a QR code here that you can scan, which will directly take you to the Amazon review page.

REVIEW US

Thank you for your support and for giving my book a chance to spark imagination, wonder, and learning in your family's lives.

Happy reading,

Riley Wolfe

Printed in Great Britain
by Amazon

60807968R00057